Intermediate | 1 Piano, 4 Hands

H★MILTON
FOR PIANO DUET

ARRANGED BY ERIC BAUMGARTNER

ISBN 978-1-70513-104-6

Visit Hal Leonard Online at
www.halleonard.com

Contact us:
Hal Leonard
7777 West Bluemound Road
Milwaukee, WI 53213
Email: info@halleonard.com

In Europe, contact:
Hal Leonard Europe Limited
42 Wigmore Street
Marylebone, London, W1U 2RN
Email: info@halleonardeurope.com

In Australia, contact:
Hal Leonard Australia Pty. Ltd.
4 Lentara Court
Cheltenham, Victoria, 3192 Australia
Email: info@halleonard.com.au

ALEXANDER HAMILTON

Words and Music by LIN-MANUEL MIRANDA
Arranged by Eric Baumgartner

DEAR THEODOSIA

Words and Music by LIN-MANUEL MIRANDA
Arranged by Eric Baumgartner

BURN

Words and Music by LIN-MANUEL MIRANDA
Arranged by Eric Baumgartner

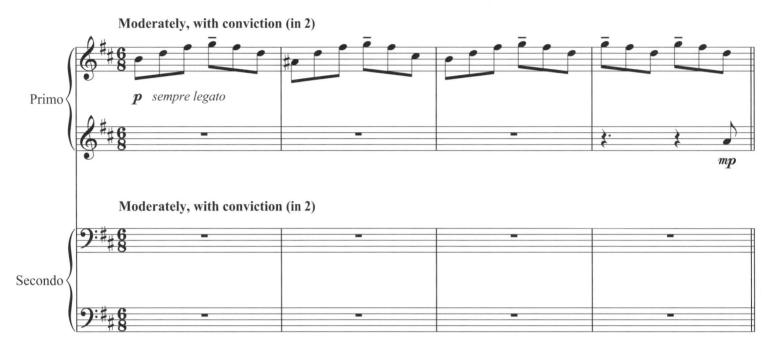

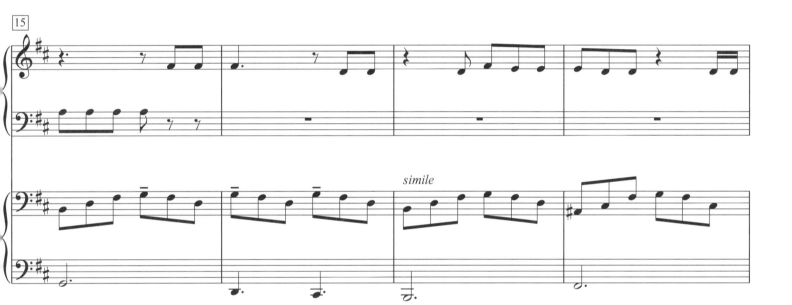

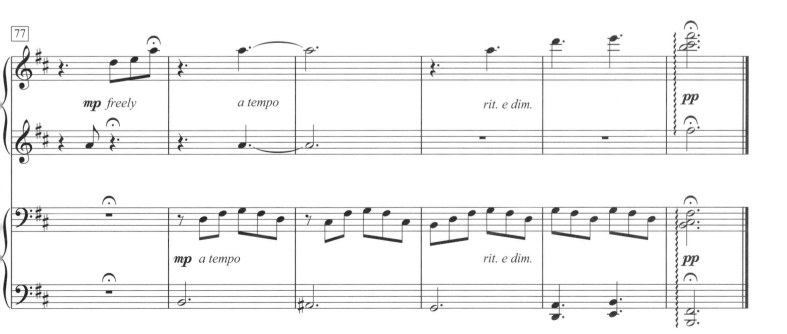

HELPLESS

Words and Music by LIN-MANUEL MIRANDA
Arranged by Eric Baumgartner

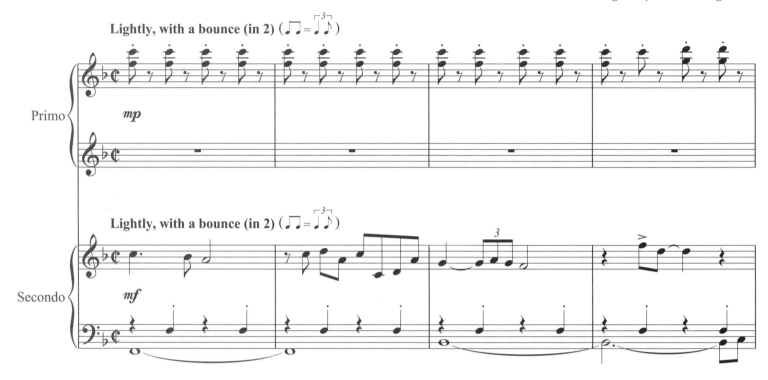

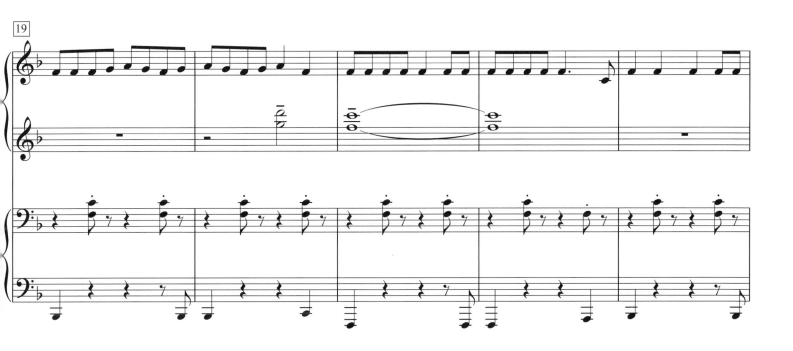

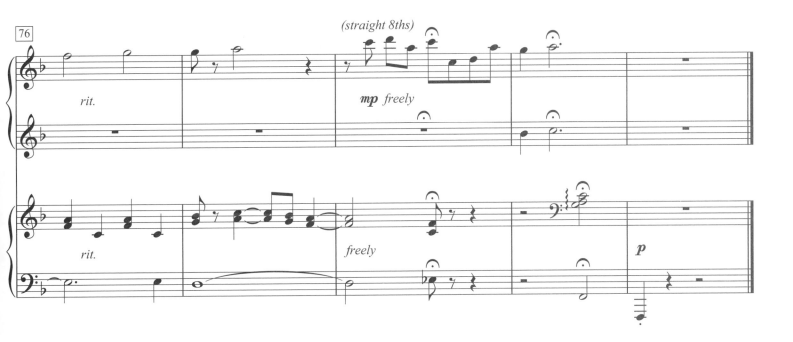

IT'S QUIET UPTOWN

Words and Music by LIN-MANUEL MIRANDA
Arranged by Eric Baumgartner

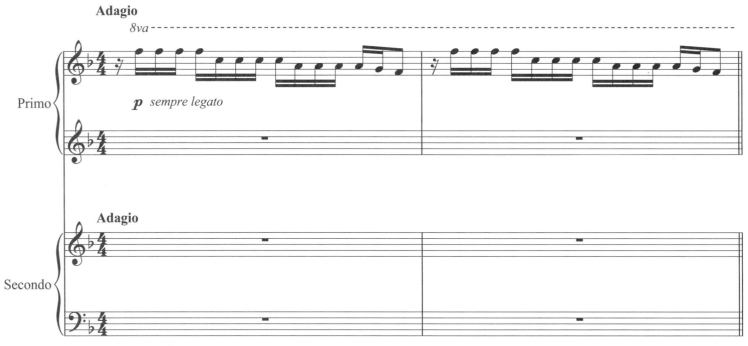

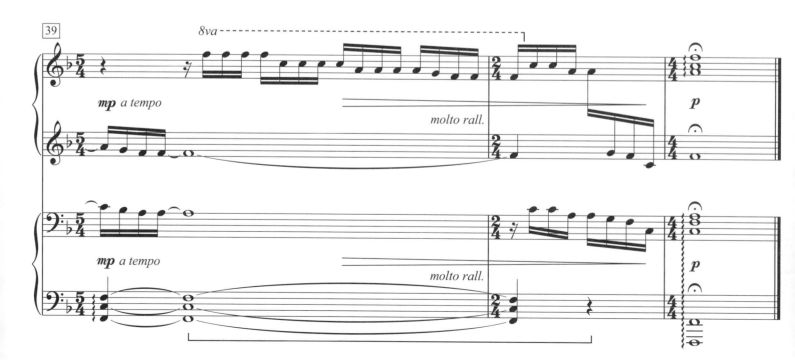

MY SHOT

Words and Music by LIN-MANUEL MIRANDA
with Albert Johnson, Kejuan Waliek Muchita,
Osten Harvey, Jr., Roger Troutman and Christopher Wallace
Arranged by Eric Baumgartner

R.H. 2nd time only

L.H. 2nd time only

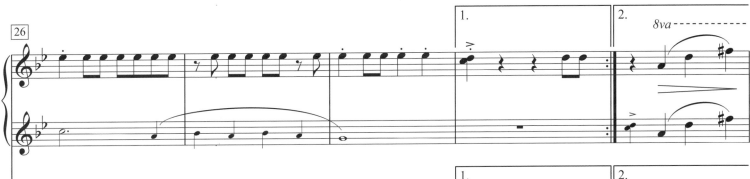

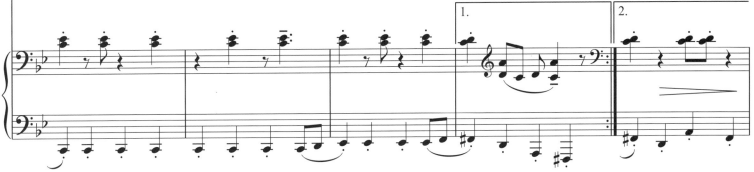

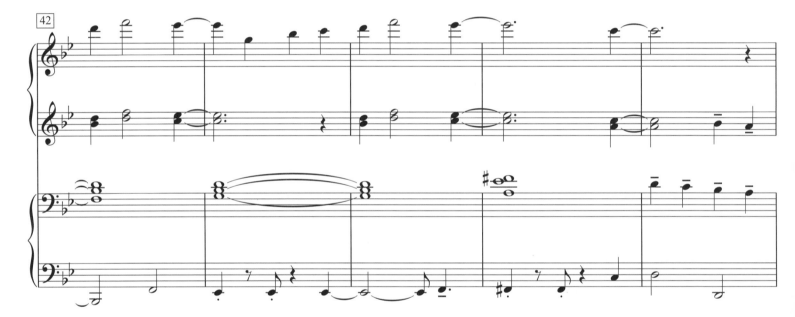

THE SCHUYLER SISTERS

Words and Music by LIN-MANUEL MIRANDA
Arranged by Eric Baumgartner

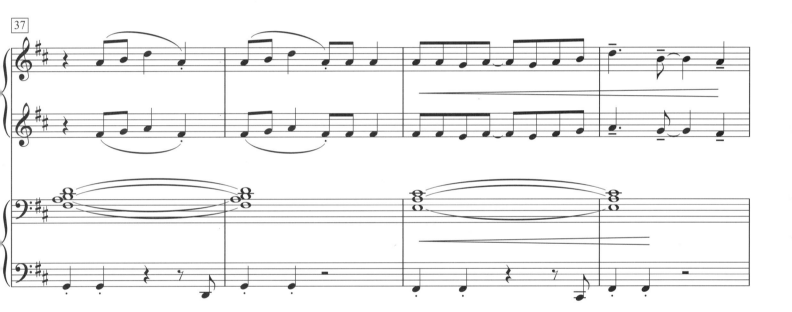

YOU'LL BE BACK

Words and Music by LIN-MANUEL MIRANDA
Arranged by Eric Baumgartner

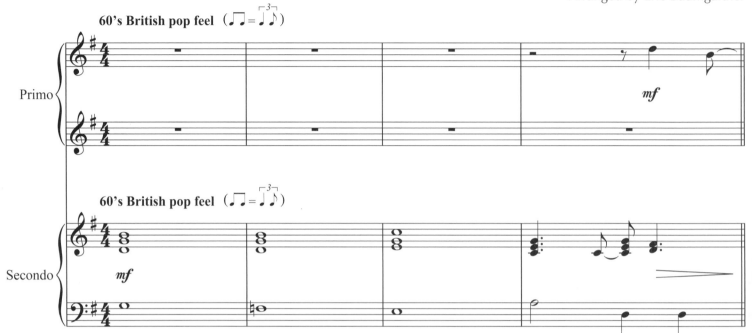

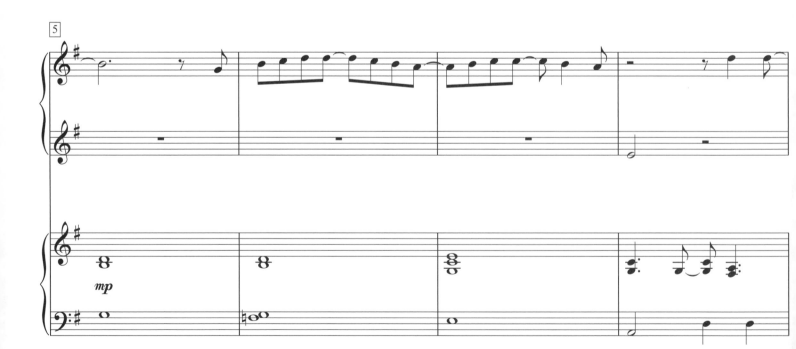

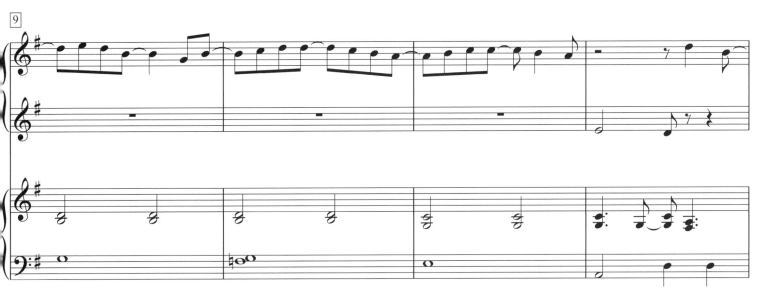